# 27 PETALS

## POEMS AND DREAMS INSPIRED BY THE SACRED HONEYBEE

Karla Michelle Capacetti-Quintana

To purchase this book in quantity contact: yogaofbeeing@gmail.com

ISBN: 9781794043862
Imprint: Independently published

1. Poetry, 2. Mind Body Spirit, 3. Beekeeping, 4. Sensuality, 5. Spirituality, 6. Dreams, 7. Honey Bees, 8. Divine Feminine

This book is dedicated to all the lovers of the world beelonging to the honeyed place where venom is also medicine.

# INVOCATION

Romancing the Hive is the greatest pleasure of my life.
I cannot hide from the omnipresent potential for pain
so I surrender to it in Her name.
Down on my knees praying at Her feet
and high in the clouds dreaming out loud.
Lost within Her landscapes I am Maiden Mother Queen
Crone.
Heartbreak found in the freedom of never being owned.
Yet I beelong to Her alone.
I am of Her moon womb comb.
I am the elusive mythstory I seek to remember.
I am the truth I search for in the dark where I let go of time
before and beyond.
May this longing never pass.
May I never betray the shadow of the Moon.
May I know full well Her newness comes from loving and
leaving and coming home again.
They may call me Her keeper but I do not claim to tame Her.
She is veil-winged wildness romancing life itself.
I am Hers forever.
For ever I am Hers.

# HAIKU FOR OUR MANY SENSES

Sharing time with Her
One comes to Remembering
Our four Bee senses

Not only can we
See Taste Listen Feel Smell Her
She helps us expand

Into Sacred *Dream*
where we *Bleed* and learn to *Heal*
love is *Love* is Love

These poems translate
The Language of OneBeeing
From deep within me

In hopes that one word
Trickles down with Honeyed Light
As inspiration

To Co-Create Truth
Our Divine Mission on Earth
Blessed Bee the Source

# CONTENTS

# SEE

# DANCING IN THE ROSES

Have you ever seen a honey bee dance
with her head in the roses?
Her body quivers as each speckle of stardust
collides within her infinite yoniverse.

As if she needed confirmation
that the sun and moon are lovers,
ours have crossed paths again.

The distance between the mountains and the sea,
the space between this moment and the next,
couldn't convince her otherwise.

Every petal is a new possibility.
Every breath into each other a new horizon.
Every buzz a new vibration.
Gently spinning the delicate thread.

Think your way through my heart
and I will feel my way through your mind.

It's only a matter of time
before we dance again.

## LOOKING FOR A MIRACLE

The shapes
have shadows
that follow them around.
You, too,
are a shape
being followed by the shadows.
They offer signs and symbols
that weave your life together
between the past and the future
and leave a path
here and now
that only you can take
to find your way home.

Don't forget to see them.
Don't forget to look.

## SECRET KEEPER

What is holding you back
from letting me hold your heart?
What secrets do you keep
hidden in the dark?
What fears have you yet to face
with your all-seeing eye?

There's nothing to gain or lose.
There's no such thing as time.
Just empty space
between your moment and mine.
That's what I'll be holding
until you're free to fly.

# TASTE

## ESSENCE

Sweet love. It's been so long since you enveloped my whole beeing. I won't take much of your time. In fact, I'll steal just one kiss and let it multiply inside me. I'm not the only one who needs to taste your heaven.

## MONSTERS & MAIDENS

There were monsters
collecting shards of broken hearts;
beautiful starving beasts
hiding beneath the bed.

Little did they know
the toll for every soul they'd beehold:
a burning crater
inside their bursting chests.

Little did they know
maidens were made to ease their plight:
taking flight for them all
storing honeylove in their dark.

Monsters need love, too.
Consume Her golden nektars;
a healing salve
from the highest source.

Don't be afraid to taste again.
Praying hearts rest on this dream pillow;
a final homecoming
to Her fertile honeycomb.

# TASTE

Last night before falling
into the realm of riddles
I asked the maker of my dreams
to offer me a taste
of the change that is upon us
as autumn reclaims this place
reflecting through my dreamtime window
she showed me you
bear skinned and bare souled
glistening with honeydew
collecting fallen twigs
gathering golden leaves
preparing our dreamtime den
mulching garden edges
pruning the budless berry bushes
that satiated your summertime hunger
you whisper magic to the maidens
as darkness takes the day
and I remember
the deliciously delightful taste
of falling into love
with you in this place.

# LISTEN

# THE BUZZ

The buzz:
a tickle in your ear;
whispers from the wings of love.

The bloom:
a smile so sweet;
kisses from the petals of light.

The dance:
a harmony you can feel;
music from the chorus of life.

This little moment:
a gift as pure as honey;
sunshine from the rays of your heart.

## PLAYING WITH FIRE

Out of sight,
out of mind.
Distant destinations keep us intertwined.
Crying out for surrendered sleep,
beeloved's beeloveds save me from me.
Too scared to know you
all,
the
way
something old begs us not to forget
backwards thinking leads to new regrets.
Baby,
baby,
baby,
crow.
Infants grow ancient as the mystery conceives.
Asking questions to the gravestone on our bed,
listening now we're the talking dead.
Confining our dreams to coffins and cribs,
mourning the loss of what could have been.
Walking away to stay ahead of the flame,
playing with fire again and again.

## DRAGONS SPEAK

While you wake I show you spaces
only the wildest creatures can navigate
as we learn to fly through life's shadowy depths

While I dream you speak to me
in languages only we can understand
as we dip into the silent waves of endless time

# FEEL

# WINGS ON FIRE

Lashes laced with gold
her eyes are mirrors to your soul
endless love beehold

Feathers scorched to black
dark soaring wings frame her back
hear hearts on fire crack

Energies align
passioned flowers intertwine
lightning fuels their veins

## SOMETHING OF THE MAGICAL

You step outside
to feel the sun
beam warmth and light
into your chest
but something feels broken inside.
An emptiness,
a darkness,
pumping pain through your veins.
You recognize it,
observe its power,
and then remember yours.
Suddenly you hear it,
the goodbye in the air.
There's no way around it
but still you chase it
because you think you aren't ready
to release and let go
but you know it's time
to release and let go.
And now you feel something new.
You're making the space
for sunbeams to break through.

# OUROBOROS

Our bodies remember the elementals that kinect us into
shapes shifting and giving into the freedom of feeling
Source course through our roots like twin serpents
uncoiling from deep sleep fueled by a pulsing fire breath
flow-ering from the furnace of the lower mouth open
and lit by the churning gears greased by tears that tear
through the cavernous depths of death where life feels
up close and persons are empowered to collide in earths
colloidal shadows exchanging energies to and fro the
upper mouth reaching higher destinations where things
are not made of metal because meddling minds make the
magician's malleable knots work harder than the
synchronized synapses sealing the chemical reactions
and electrical attractions that bring us closer to
becoming the mechanics and the pressure to perform
dissolves in the potential to transform nuts and bolts
into quantum lips and curious fingertips that trick the
tail into eating itself again entering infinity renewed.

# SMELL

## TAKE YOUR LOSSES IN THE FALL (SMOKE SIGNALS)

We prayed about this day
unsure of the outcome
certain of the risk
gentle steps approach
her castle made of gold
offerings of gratitude
from the rootstar of the Earth

White smoke signals change
sisters reawaken to Great Mother in peril
daughters crawl in search of the Source
goddesses soar through the autumn sky

Compassion consumes them all
disruption free of fear
resignation full of love
sacrifice for the good of the whole

Angel fallen never forgotten
her life shines light in dark places
her heart beats an eternal rhythm
her crown reigns true forever

## PROPOLIS

It's been on the tip of her tongue
since he left it there a million years ago;
the familiar scent of a city up in flames.

Strangers come and go finding temporary home,
while the alchemist paves his city streets,
turning their lead dust into golden embers.

He will build this city and he will burn this city,
again and again, until his search reveals
every landscape that came before it.

Her shadows dance into the smoke
and he inhales the medicine
she foraged from the forests,
blended with the blossoms,
and mingled with the minerals.

This city is built with her essence.

Every time it burns, she memorizes
the taste he has forgotten
and breathes it back into him.

# GRATITUDE

This goes without saying. But, it's you. It's always
been you. The warm touch that comforts on a chilled
morning. The cool breeze that whispers in the air. The
brilliant light that feeds heavy hearts. The resilient
roots that ground the strongest will. The more-than-
pleasant perfume that fills infinite space. The passing
time that stands still within each precious moment.
The passionate voice that sings Grace into Life. The
silent knowing that all is perfection. The simple truth
that only love can win. It's you.

It's always been you.

# DREAM

# BEECOMING

Altaring my reality
Trusting my truth
Honoring my death
Birthing my life
Building my comb
Making my home
Surrendering my fear
Finding my flow
Ripening my fruits
Deepening my roots
Scattering my seed
Beecoming my dream

## STAR GATE

Like shapes on a map,
we've drawn the millions of miracles
that have made their way
across the landscapes of our tender hearts.

Like virgin honeycomb,
we've erased the imaginary boundaries
that have kept our souls
from melting in a sweet and endless flow.

Like children in a new world,
we've explored the timely truths
that have helped us remember
how to dream between the realms.

# DIVINING DUALITY

This one is for you.
And you, and you, and you.
Because you keep shifting, changing.
Transforming your appearance.
One day you're a garden.
The next you are a desert.
One night you're the apple.
The next you are the sand.
In one breath you're a serpent and a mirage.
In one dream you're a treasure and a secret.

One thousand faces.
Ten thousand names.

Still I know your hero heart remains the same.
Each new moment is a lesson in the making.
Each new vision is a reflection in the mirror.

Let me bee, your humble student.
Let me bee, your infinite counterpart.

# BLEED

## SALVAGE

My womb birthed an ocean
your song brought the tide
our love built a ship

Even when it's heartwrecked
we keep searching
each enchanted island
for our washed-up pearls
lit by a moon on fire
dancing in the water
salvaging our truth

## RED MOON BAPTISM

Goddess bless
cleanse any and all unrest
let your frigid waters flow freely through my chest
I come to you for holy sacrament
three dips deep
anoint my crown, hips, & feet
attune to maiden, mother, queen, crone
atone for past, present, future, unknown
I have nothing but myself to give
please accept as offering
a heart song from my drumming moon
the rose blood from my virgin womb
receive me in love
regenerate me infinitely
take me home in peace

## 27 PETALS

They all come to bee
in their own time.
The first to awaken as a bud,
the first to wither on the bush.

Oh honey,
let my petals fall away,
each and every one.
Let the fruit that's ripe to pick
be the first to taste rebirth.
In these seeds you'll find
wisdom for Earth's family.

# HEAL

WOUNDED

Darling,
I know your heart is brittle, too.
This perfect chase has worn us out
like two loose ends of a single thread.

Let's pour our souls into the Sun
feel the golden nectar flow.
Drip by drip our aching hearts
will quench a universal thirst.

Let the Earth weave Her roots
between every gentle breathe
till we can't tell where your scars end
and mine seem to begin.

## WARRIOR HEART

They wrapped you tightly in a silky snakeskin garment
and I danced as you shed their outdated layers.

They covered you entirely in a cold and frigid blizzard
and I burned as you stepped through the flames.

They muffled you shut in a dark and rusty drum
and I listened as you made music out of the deadly silence.

They drowned you out in a pocket full of seashells
and I breathed as you plunged deeper into the darkness.

They held you down in a heavy winded blow
and I swirled as you flew higher rising like a phoenix.

You learn to love them all and come home to show me how
your warrior heart keeps healing,
growing stronger with each scar.

## MEDICINE KEEPERS

The Queen devotes her days
to disseminating divine Drone medicine.
Her Pharaohmones navigating the nest
giving life to magic-making Maidens.

With every flight they imbibe
spirits and libations and a fructiferous invitation,
carrying their consenting confectionary consorts
home to where the healing happens.

Within the hexagonal moonwombcomb
OneBeeing directs the mystic rituals,
priestess sisters gestate sacred juices,
birthing an abundant annual apothecary.

Daughters curate spring nectars,
summer songs and autumn herbals
so that in the darkest winter Moon
they'll embody all the medicine of the Son.

# LOVE

## LOVE REMEMBERED

You are a creature of wonder. I wonder if you remember
    making love to me here.

At the river that weaves her creeks through the cracks of
    our ancient volcanic hearts.

On the mountain that hosts the songs of queens and
    kings feeding the soul of the soil.

In the clouds that fog the view of a million memories just
    dying to shine through.

Your brief and tender embrace carries me through the
    cosmic forest of our forgotten dreams.

We've made love here before. We'll make love here again
    and again until we finally remember
        all the wonders of our creation.

## THE OFFERING

Church and childhood
linger on the periphery
siesta in the sun
afternoon service
collection
connection
congregation
massive visionary virgins
stingless and fecund
brothers not yet fathers
chosen ones embark
a hero's quest
to crown the queen
flying
falling
phallus
greater sacrament
never taken
always freely given
an offering
from angels
in the loft

## MER-KA-BA

I came here to find you
on the spiral journey
I found myself
shapeshifting
beetwixt and beetween
twin helix realms
like one synchronized soul
experiencing two syncopated bodies
searching for fractals of the other
reveiled by messengers
traveling in reverse
chasing future memories
I've scaled mountains of moonlight
guided by kaleidoscopes
in hopes that we exist on infinite planes
somewhere in the chaos
where the colors bleed together
every verse inscribed is a dream
piercing the silver line
every dream incubated is poetry
waiting to be liberated
free falling keeps me grounded
the distance doesn't phase me

my desire encapsulates the whole
a container that fits the silence
between the notes
beeloved I can hear you
never fear that I'm not near you
surrendering to the same sacred spirals

**Karla Michelle Capacetti-Quintana** has been practicing Sacred Beekeeping since 2015, though the spirit of OneBeeing has been present in her life since childhood. On the cusp of her 27th golden birthday she visited Joshua Tree, California to be initiated into the Way of the Melissae teachings within the Path of Pollen where she experienced life altering revelations that have progressively become integrated into her beeing. Since then, she has immersed herself in a program of self-study, allowing the honey bees, their bioregional plant allies, and their OneBeeing Spirit to guide her on the beauty way.

As a self-taught herbalist, student at the College of the Melissae, seeker on the Path of Pollen, and a yoga teacher and practitioner, Karla uses her intuition to tune her many senses towards the archetype of OneBeeing to fulfill her life mission of midwifing the Earth and all of her children into in a new world and way of beeing. Blessed Bee!

Made in the USA
Columbia, SC
15 January 2021

31056793R00029